PIANO • VOCAL • GUITAR   THE **BIG BOOK** OF   3RD EDITION

MOVIE MUSIC

ISBN 978-1-5400-2003-1

7777 W. BLUEMOUND RD. P.O. BOX 13819 MILWAUKEE, WI 53213

For all works contained herein:
Unauthorized copying, arranging, adapting, recording, Internet posting, public performance,
or other distribution of the printed music in this publication is an infringement of copyright.
Infringers are liable under the law.

Visit Hal Leonard Online at
www.halleonard.com

CONTENTS

ALL FOR LOVE

from THE THREE MUSKETEERS

Words and Music by BRYAN ADAMS,
R.J. LANGE and MICHAEL KAMEN

Moderately, not too fast

When it's love you give, ___ (I'll be a man of good
___ (I swear I'll al-ways be
___ (I'll be the fire in your

faith.) then in love you'll live. ___ (I'll make a stand. I won't break.)
strong.) then there's a rea-son why. ___ (I'll prove to you we be-long.)
night.) then it's love you take. ___ (I will de-fend, I will fight.)

I'll be the rock you can build on, ___
I'll be the wall that pro-tects you ___
I'll be there when you need me. ___

Copyright © 1993 Wonderland Music Company, Inc., Sony/ATV Music Publishing LLC, K-Man Corp., Badams Music Ltd. and Out Of Pocket Productions Ltd.
All Rights on behalf of Sony/ATV Music Publishing LLC and K-Man Corp. Administered by Sony/ATV Music Publishing LLC, 424 Church Street, Suite 1200, Nashville, TN 37219
All Rights on behalf of Out Of Pocket Productions Ltd. Administered by Universal - PolyGram International Publishing, Inc.
International Copyright Secured   All Rights Reserved

AMERICA
from the Motion Picture THE JAZZ SINGER

Words and Music by
NEIL DIAMOND

Moderately bright

Far,   we've been trav - el - ing far, __

with - out __ a home, __

but not with-out a star. __

Copyright © 1980 STONEBRIDGE-MUSIC, INC.
All Rights Administered by UNIVERSAL TUNES
All Rights Reserved   Used by Permission

Ev - 'ry-where a - round ___ the world,

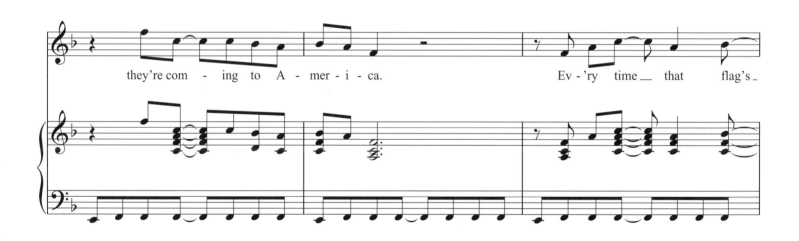

they're com - ing to A - mer - i - ca.   Ev - 'ry time ___ that   flag's _

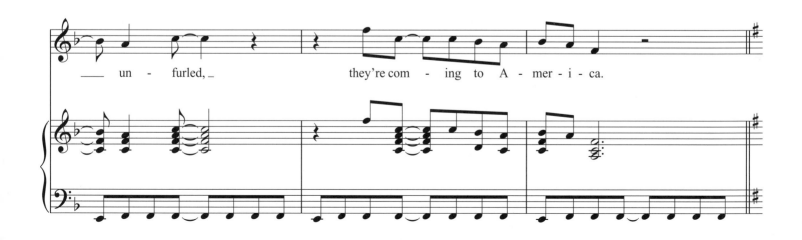

___ un - furled, _   they're com - ing to A - mer - i - ca.

AND ALL THAT JAZZ
from CHICAGO

Words by FRED EBB
Music by JOHN KANDER

© 1975 (Renewed) KANDER & EBB INC. and UNICHAPPELL MUSIC INC.
All Rights Administered by UNICHAPPELL MUSIC INC.
All Rights Reserved   Used by Permission

No, I'm no one's wife,_ but oh, I

love my life_ and all _____ that _____

_ jazz! _____ That jazz!

BACK TO THE FUTURE

from the Universal Motion Picture BACK TO THE FUTURE

By ALAN SILVESTRI

Copyright © 1985 USI B MUSIC PUBLISHING
All Rights Controlled and Administered by SONGS OF UNIVERSAL, INC.
All Rights Reserved   Used by Permission

BEAUTY AND THE BEAST
from BEAUTY AND THE BEAST

Music by ALAN MENKEN
Lyrics by HOWARD ASHMAN

© 1991 Wonderland Music Company, Inc. and Walt Disney Music Company
All Rights Reserved. Used by Permission.

BELLA'S LULLABY
from the Summit Entertainment film TWILIGHT

By CARTER BURWELL

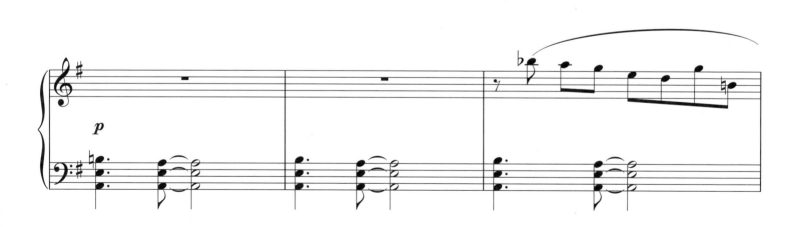

© 2008 WB MUSIC CORP.
All Rights Reserved   Used by Permission

BLAZE OF GLORY

featured in the film YOUNG GUNS II

Words and Music by
JON BON JOVI

wake up   in the morn - ing and I   raise my wea - ry head, ___   I've got an
night I go to bed,   I pray the Lord my soul   to keep. _   No, I ain't

Copyright © 1990, 1992 Bon Jovi Publishing
All Rights Administered by Kobalt Songs Music Publishing
All Rights Reserved   Used by Permission

CANDLE ON THE WATER

from PETE'S DRAGON

Words and Music by AL KASHA
and JOEL HIRSCHHORN

I'll be your can-dle on the wa-ter,

{ my love for you will al-ways
{ 'til ev-'ry wave is warm and

burn.   I know you're lost   and drift-ing,   but the clouds are lift-ing.
bright.   My soul is there   be-side you,   let this can-dle guide you;

Don't give up; you have some-where to turn.
soon you'll see a gold-en stream of light.

© 1976 Walt Disney Music Company and Wonderland Music Company, Inc.
Copyright Renewed.
All Rights Reserved. Used by Permission.

CITY OF STARS
from LA LA LAND

Music by JUSTIN HURWITZ
Lyrics by BENJ PASEK
& JUSTIN PAUL

Sebastian: Cit - y of stars, _ are you shin - ing just for me?

Cit - y of stars, _

there's so much that I can't see. Who

© 2016 Justin Hurwitz Music (BMI), B Lion Music (BMI), and Warner-Tamerlane Publishing Corp. (BMI), all administered by Warner-Tamerlane Publishing Corp. (BMI)/
Pick In A Pinch Music (ASCAP), breathelike music (ASCAP), A Lion Music (ASCAP), and WB Music Corp. (ASCAP), all administered by WB Music Corp. (ASCAP)
All Rights Reserved   Used by Permission

CINEMA PARADISO
from CINEMA PARADISO

By ENNIO MORRICONE
and ANDREA MORRICONE

Simply, with feeling

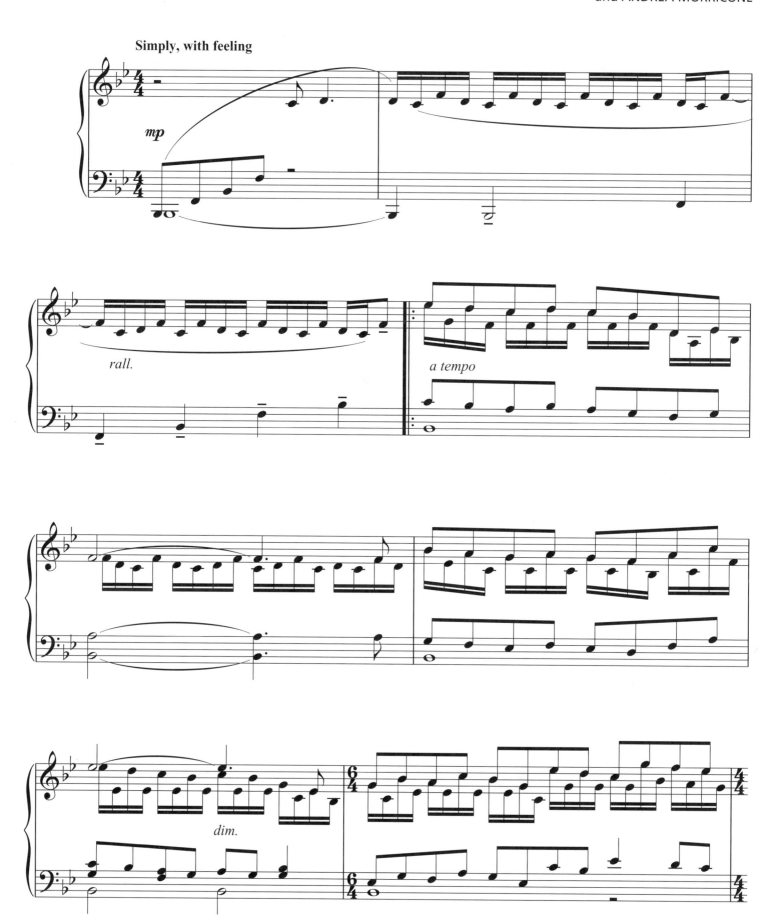

Copyright © 1988 EMI General Music SRL
All Rights Administered by Sony/ATV Music Publishing LLC, 424 Church Street, Suite 1200, Nashville, TN 37219
International Copyright Secured   All Rights Reserved

53

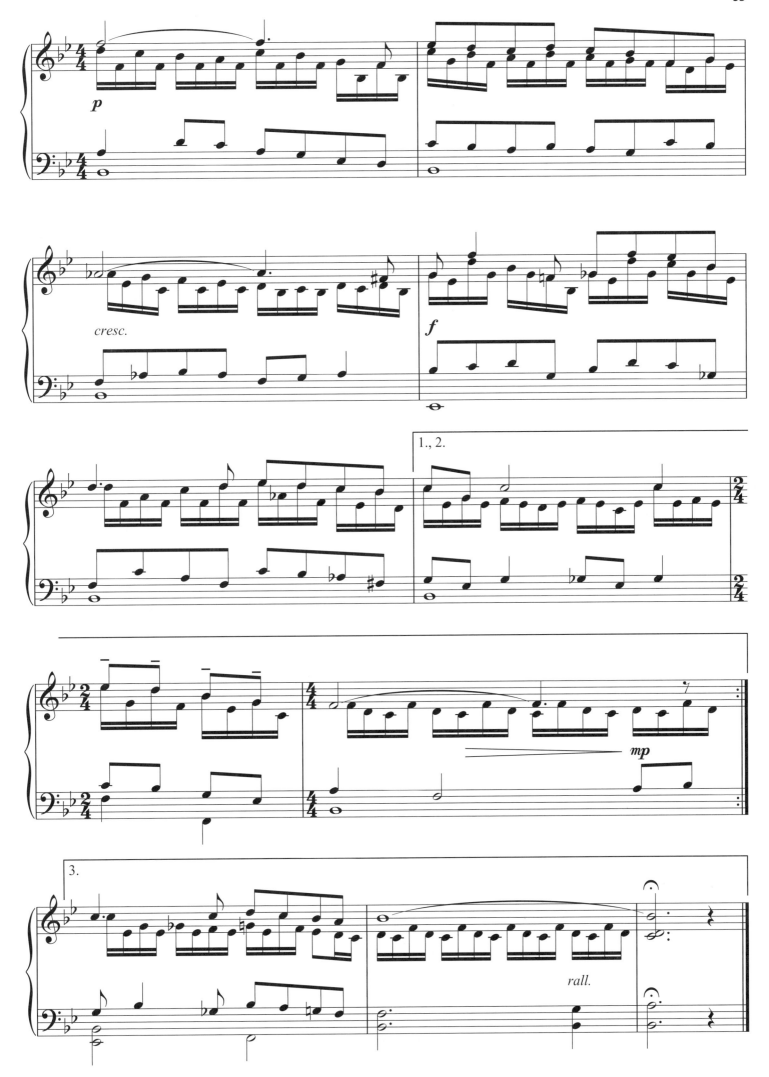

COLORS OF THE WIND
from POCAHONTAS

Music by ALAN MENKEN
Lyrics by STEPHEN SCHWARTZ

© 1995 Wonderland Music Company, Inc. and Walt Disney Music Company
All Rights Reserved. Used by Permission.

CUPS
(When I'm Gone)
from the Motion Picture Soundtrack PITCH PERFECT

Words and Music by A.P. CARTER,
LUISA GERSTEIN and HELOISE TUNSTALL-BEHRENS

Moderate Folk

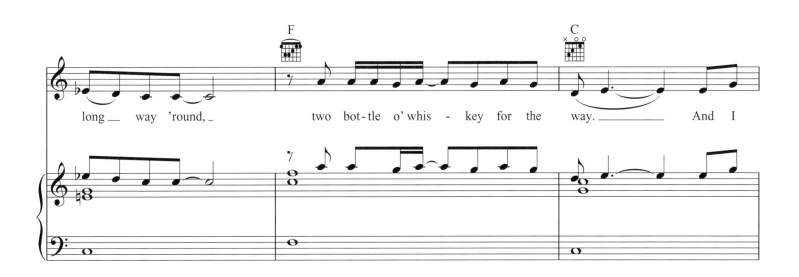

Copyright © 2013 by Peer International Corporation and BMG Gold Songs
All Rights for BMG Gold Songs Administered by BMG Rights Management (US) LLC
International Copyright Secured All Rights Reserved
- contains a sample from "When I'm Gone" by A.P. Carter

DAWN
from PRIDE AND PREJUDICE

By DARIO MARIANELLI

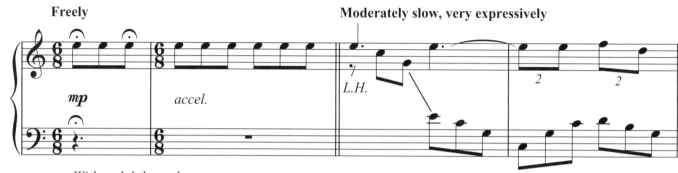

With pedal throughout

Copyright © 2005 UNIVERSAL PICTURES MUSIC
All Rights Controlled and Administered by UNIVERSAL MUSIC CORP.
All Rights Reserved   Used by Permission

Moderately fast, with motion

THE ENGLISH PATIENT
from THE ENGLISH PATIENT

Written by
GABRIEL YARED

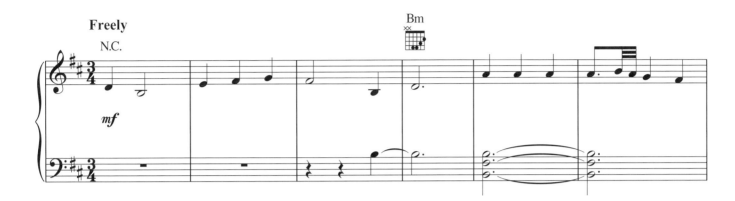

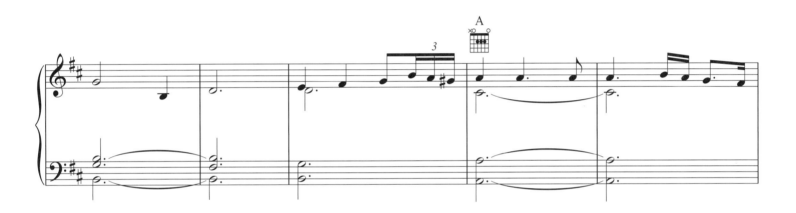

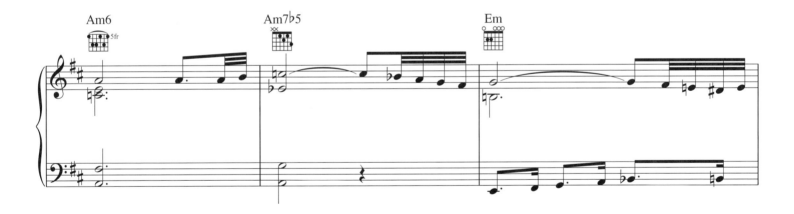

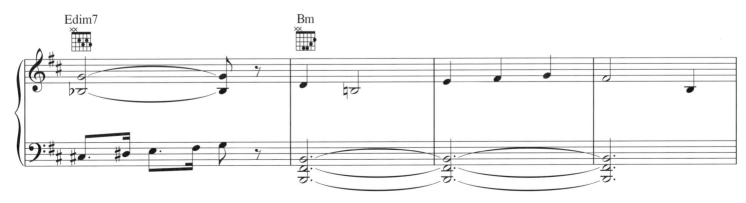

Copyright © 1996 by Tiger Moth Music
International Copyright Secured   All Rights Reserved

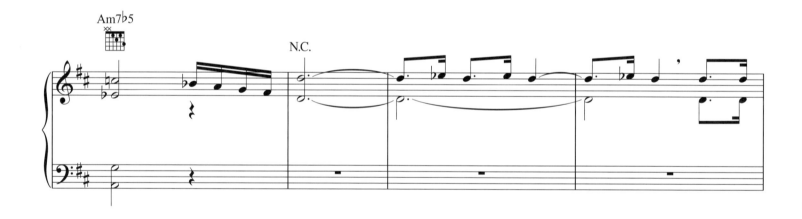

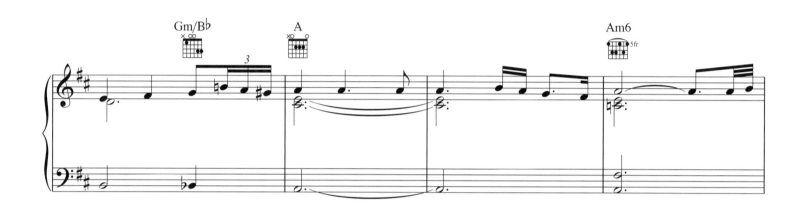

DAYS OF WINE AND ROSES

from DAYS OF WINE AND ROSES

Lyric by JOHNNY MERCER
Music by HENRY MANCINI

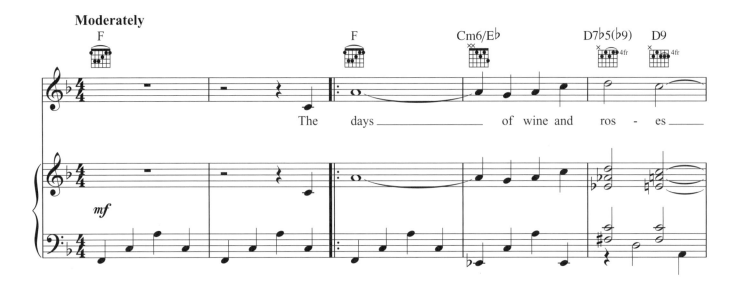

The days _____ of wine and ros - es _____

_____ laugh and run a - way _____ like a child at play, _____ through the

mead - ow - land to - ward a clos - ing door, a door marked "Nev - er - more," that

© 1962 (Renewed) WB MUSIC CORP. and THE JOHNNY MERCER FOUNDATION
All Rights Administered by WB MUSIC CORP.
All Rights Reserved   Used by Permission

DO YOU KNOW WHERE YOU'RE GOING TO?

Theme from MAHOGANY

Music and Lyrics by GERRY GOFFIN
and MICHAEL MASSER

Copyright © 1973 Screen Gems-EMI Music Inc. and Jobete Music Co., Inc.
Copyright Renewed
All Rights Administered by Sony/ATV Music Publishing LLC, 424 Church Street, Suite 1200, Nashville, TN 37219
International Copyright Secured   All Rights Reserved

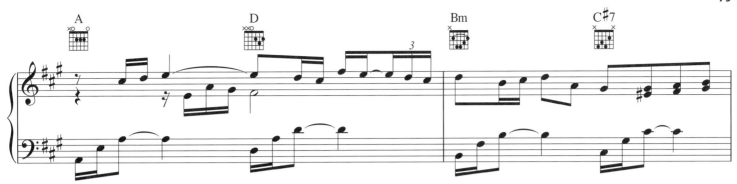

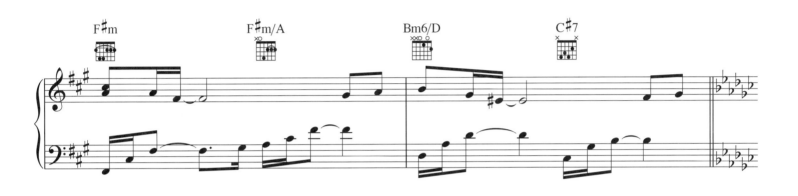

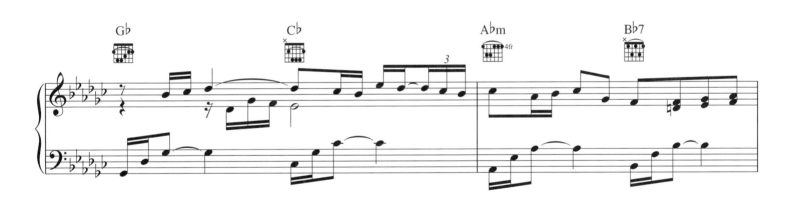

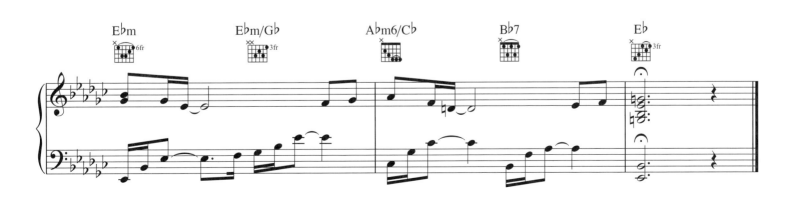

ENDLESS LOVE

from ENDLESS LOVE

Words and Music by
LIONEL RICHIE

Copyright © 1981 by PGP Music, Brockman Music and Brenda Richie Publishing
All Rights for PGP Music Administered by Intersong U.S.A., Inc.
International Copyright Secured   All Rights Reserved

THEME FROM E.T.
(The Extra-Terrestrial)
from the Universal Picture E.T. (THE EXTRA-TERRESTRIAL)

Music by JOHN WILLIAMS

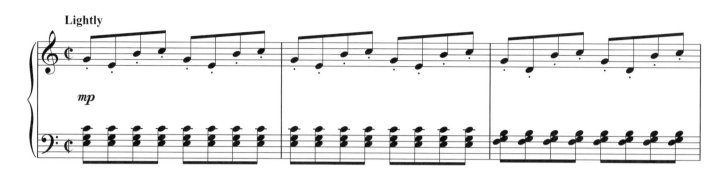

Copyright © 1982 USI B MUSIC PUBLISHING
All Rights Controlled and Administered by SONGS OF UNIVERSAL, INC.
All Rights Reserved   Used by Permission

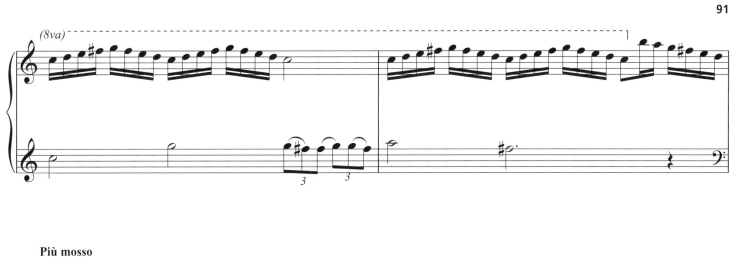

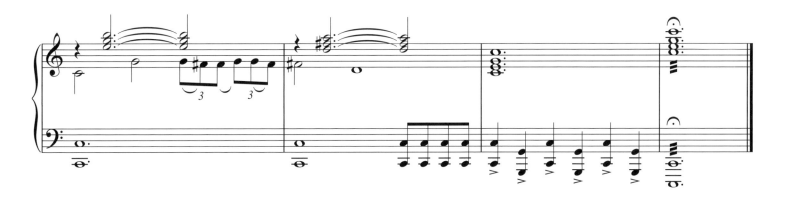

EXHALE
(Shoop Shoop)
from the Original Soundtrack Album WAITING TO EXHALE

Words and Music by
BABYFACE

Easy R&B Ballad

(1.) Ev - 'ry - one falls in love some - times. _____ Some - times it's
(2., 3.) laugh, some - times you'll cry. _____ Life nev - er

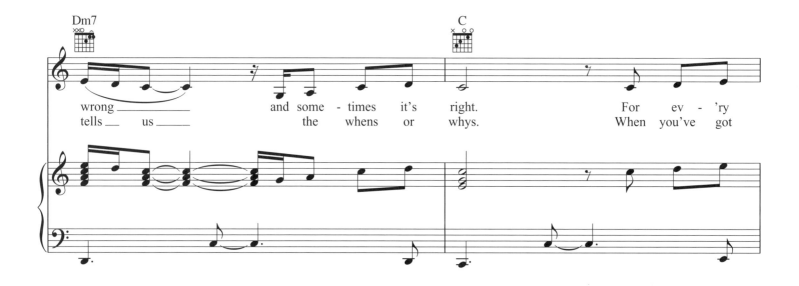

wrong _____ and some - times it's right. For ev - 'ry
tells _ us _____ the whens or whys. When you've got

win some - one must fail, but there comes a
friends to wish you well, you'll find a

Copyright © 1995 Sony/ATV Music Publishing LLC, ECAF Music and Fox Film Music Corporation
All Rights on behalf of Sony/ATV Music Publishing LLC and ECAF Music Administered by Sony/ATV Music Publishing LLC, 424 Church Street, Suite 1200, Nashville, TN 37219
International Copyright Secured   All Rights Reserved

FOR ALL WE KNOW

from the Motion Picture LOVERS AND OTHER STRANGERS

Words by ROBB WILSON and ARTHUR JAMES
Music by FRED KARLIN

Copyright © 1970 UNIVERSAL MUSIC CORP. and SONGS OF UNIVERSAL, INC.
Copyright Renewed
All Rights Reserved   Used by Permission

EYE OF THE TIGER

Theme from ROCKY III

Words and Music by FRANK SULLIVAN
and JIM PETERIK

Copyright © 1982 Sony/ATV Music Publishing LLC, Rude Music, Three Wise Boys LLC, WB Music Corp. and Easy Action Music
All Rights on behalf of Sony/ATV Music Publishing LLC, Rude Music and Three Wise Boys LLC Administered by Sony/ATV Music Publishing LLC, 424 Church Street, Suite 1200, Nashville, TN 37219
All Rights on behalf of Easy Action Music Administered by WB Music Corp.
International Copyright Secured   All Rights Reserved

So man-y times __ it hap-pens too fast. __
Face to face, __ out in the heat, __
Ris-in' up, __ straight to the top. __

You trade your pas-sion for glo - ry.
hang-in' tough, stay-in' hun - gry.
Had the guts, got the glo - ry.

Don't lose your grip __ on the
They stack the odds, __ still we
Went the dis - tance. Now I'm

dreams of the past. You must fight just to keep them a - live.
take to the street for the kill with the skill to sur - vive. __
not gon - na stop, just a man and his will to sur - vive. __

FALLING SLOWLY
from the Motion Picture ONCE

Words and Music by GLEN HANSARD
and MARKETA IRGLOVA

© 2006 THE SWELL SEASON PUBLISHING
All Rights Administered by WB MUSIC CORP.
Exclusive Worldwide Print Rights Administered by ALFRED MUSIC
All Rights Reserved   Used by Permission

now you're gone. ___

FLASHDANCE...WHAT A FEELING

from the Paramount Picture FLASHDANCE

Words by KEITH FORSEY and IRENE CARA
Music by GIORGIO MORODER

© 1983 WB MUSIC CORP., SONY/ATV HARMONY, ALCOR MUSIC (USA) and CARUB MUSIC
All Rights Administered by WB MUSIC CORP.
All Rights Reserved   Used by Permission

FOR THE FIRST TIME

from ONE FINE DAY

Words and Music by JAMES NEWTON HOWARD,
JUD FRIEDMAN and ALLAN RICH

Moderately slow

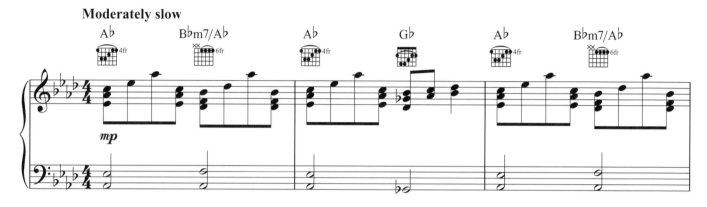

Are those your eyes? Is ___ that your smile? I've been
real? Can ___ this be true? Am I the

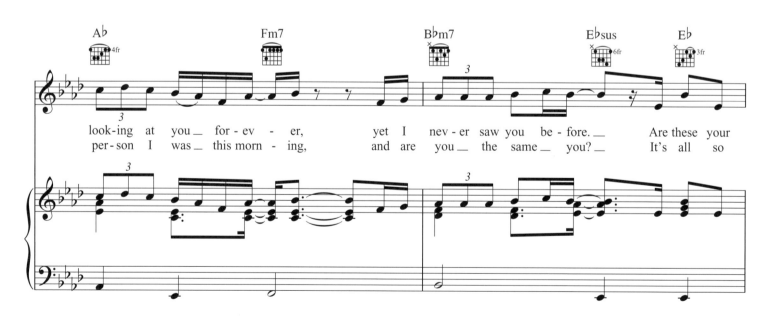

look-ing at you ___ for-ev-er, yet I nev-er saw you be-fore. ___ Are these your
per-son I was ___ this morn-ing, and are you ___ the same ___ you? ___ It's all so

Copyright © 1996 Big Fig Music, EMI Music Publishing Ltd., Schmoogie Tunes, T C F Music Publishing, Inc. and Spirit Catalogue Holdings, S.a.r.l.
All Rights on behalf of Big Fig Music and EMI Music Publishing Ltd. Administered by Sony/ATV Music Publishing LLC, 424 Church Street, Suite 1200, Nashville, TN 37219
All Rights on behalf of Schmoogie Tunes Administered by Peermusic Ltd.
All Rights on behalf of Spirit Catalogue Holdings, S.a.r.l. Administered by Spirit Two Music, Inc.
International Copyright Secured   All Rights Reserved

A HARD DAY'S NIGHT
from A HARD DAY'S NIGHT

Words and Music by JOHN LENNON
and PAUL McCARTNEY

Moderately, with a beat

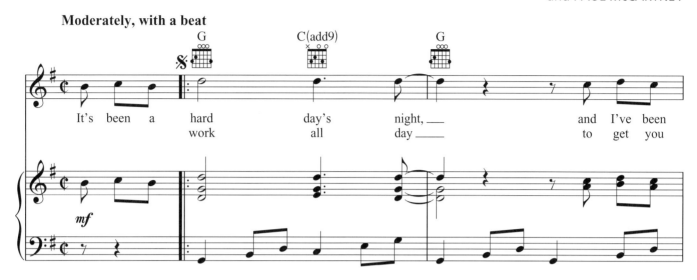

It's been a hard day's night, ___ and I've been
work all day ___ to get you

work-ing like a dog. ___ It's been a hard day's night, ___
mon-ey to buy your things. ___ And it's worth it just to hear you say ___

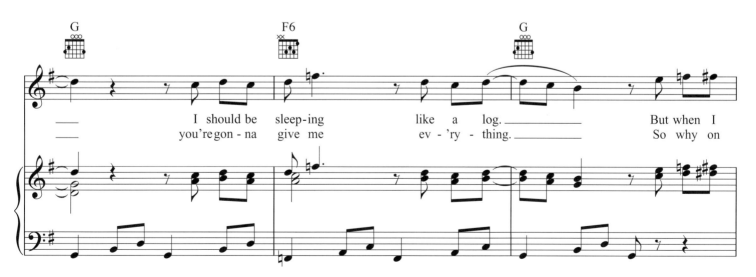

___ I should be sleep-ing like a log. ___ But when I
___ you're gon-na give me ev-'ry-thing. ___ So why on

Copyright © 1964 Sony/ATV Music Publishing LLC
Copyright Renewed
All Rights Administered by Sony/ATV Music Publishing LLC, 424 Church Street, Suite 1200, Nashville, TN 37219
International Copyright Secured   All Rights Reserved

126

HOW FAR I'LL GO

(Alessia Cara Version)
from MOANA

Music and Lyrics by
LIN-MANUEL MIRANDA

© 2016 Walt Disney Music Company
All Rights Reserved. Used by Permission.

I FINALLY FOUND SOMEONE

from THE MIRROR HAS TWO FACES

Words and Music by BARBRA STREISAND,
MARVIN HAMLISCH, R.J. LANGE
and BRYAN ADAMS

Copyright © 1996 Emanuel Music, ole Team Sports Music, Out Of Pocket Productions Ltd. and Badams Music Ltd.
All Rights on behalf of ole Team Sports Music Administered by Sony/ATV Music Publishing LLC, 424 Church Street, Suite 1200, Nashville, TN 37219
All Rights on behalf of Out Of Pocket Productions Ltd. in the United States and Canada Administered by Universal - PolyGram International Publishing, Inc.
International Copyright Secured   All Rights Reserved

I SAY A LITTLE PRAYER

featured in the TriStar Motion Picture MY BEST FRIEND'S WEDDING

Lyric by HAL DAVID
Music by BURT BACHARACH

Moderately fast

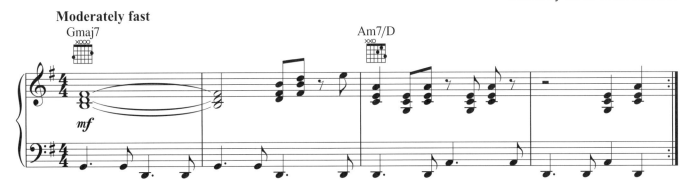

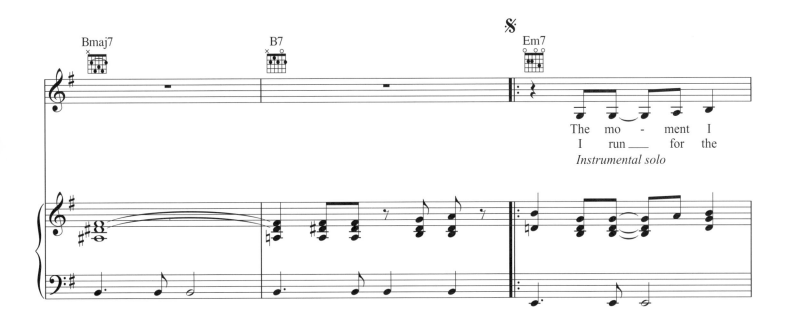

The mo - ment I
I run ___ for the
Instrumental solo

wake up,
bus, dear.

be - fore ___ I put
While rid - ing, I

on my
think of

make - up,
us, dear.

I I
(I

Copyright © 1966 BMG Rights Management (UK) Ltd., Songs Of Fujimusic and New Hidden Valley Music Co.
Copyright Renewed
All Rights Administered by BMG Rights Management (US) LLC
All Rights Reserved   Used by Permission

I WALK THE LINE

featured in WALK THE LINE

Words and Music by
JOHN R. CASH

Copyright © 1956 House Of Cash, Inc.
Copyright Renewed
All Rights in the U.S. Administered by BMG Rights Management (US) LLC
All Rights outside the U.S. Administered by Unichappell Music Inc.
All Rights Reserved   Used by Permission

Additional Lyrics

3. As sure as night is dark and day is light,
   I keep you on my mind both day and night.
   And happiness I've known proves that it's right.
   Because you're mine I walk the line.

4. You've got a way to keep me on your side.
   You give me cause for love that I can't hide.
   For you I know I'd even try to turn the tide.
   Because you're mine I walk the line.

5. I keep a close watch on this heart of mine.
   I keep my eyes wide open all the time.
   I keep the ends out for the tie that binds.
   Because you're mine I walk the line.

I WILL FOLLOW HIM
(I Will Follow You)
featured in the Motion Picture SISTER ACT

English Words by NORMAN GIMBEL and ARTHUR ALTMAN
French Words by JACQUES PLANTE
Music by J.W. STOLE and DEL ROMA

Moderately, with a beat

Copyright © 1962, 1963 by LES EDITIONS JACQUE PLANTE, Paris, France
Copyright Renewed
English Lyric Assigned to WORDS WEST LLC (P.O. Box 15187, Beverly Hills, CA 90209 USA) for the world
English Lyric Version Administered by UNIVERSAL MUSIC CORP. and WORDS WEST LLC for the U.S. and Canada
All Rights Reserved   Used by Permission

IT MIGHT AS WELL BE SPRING

from STATE FAIR

Lyrics by OSCAR HAMMERSTEIN II
Music by RICHARD RODGERS

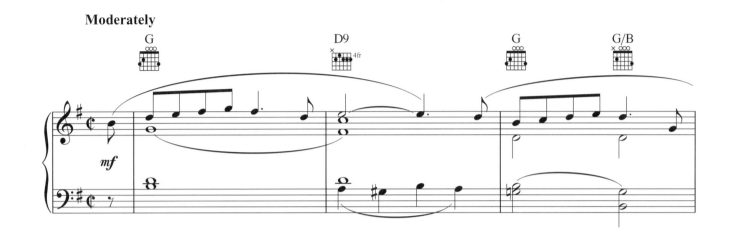

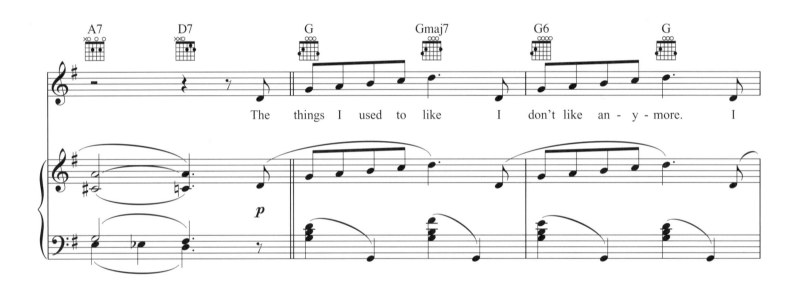

The things I used to like I don't like an-y-more. I want a lot of oth-er things I've

nev-er had be-fore. It's just like moth-er

Copyright © 1945 by Williamson Music, a Division of Rodgers & Hammerstein: an Imagem Company
Copyright Renewed
International Copyright Secured   All Rights Reserved

154

IT MIGHT BE YOU
Theme from TOOTSIE

Words by ALAN and MARILYN BERGMAN
Music by DAVE GRUSIN

© 1982 EMI GOLD HORIZON MUSIC CORP. and EMI GOLDEN TORCH MUSIC CORP.
Exclusive Worldwide Print Rights Administered by ALFRED MUSIC
All Rights Reserved   Used by Permission

THEME FROM "JAWS"
from the Universal Picture JAWS

By JOHN WILLIAMS

Very steady and threatening

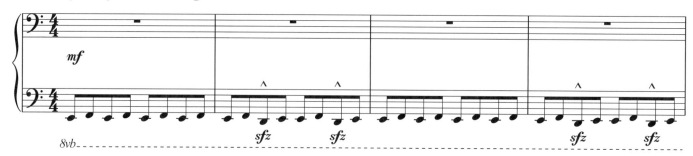

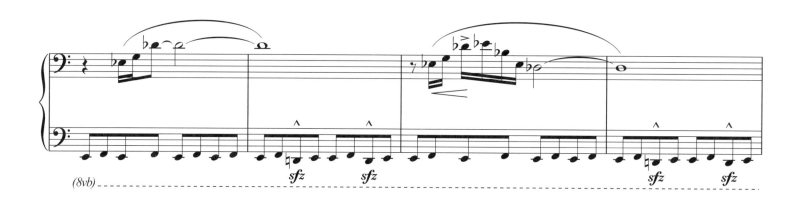

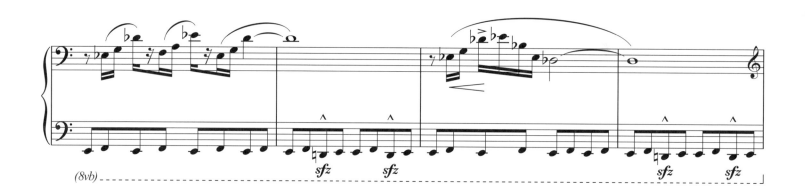

More flowing

Copyright © 1975 USI B MUSIC PUBLISHING
Copyright Renewed
All Rights Controlled and Administered by SONGS OF UNIVERSAL, INC.
All Rights Reserved   Used by Permission

Repeat and Fade

THE JOHN DUNBAR THEME
from DANCES WITH WOLVES

By JOHN BARRY

Moderately

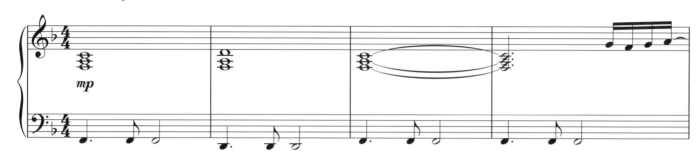

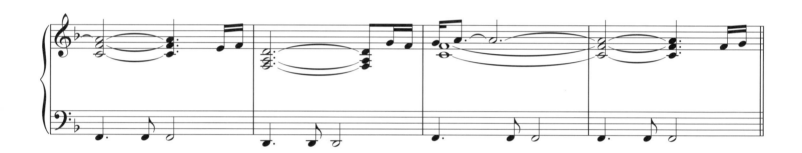

Copyright © 1990 EMI Blackwood Music Inc., Affirmed Music and Donna Dijon Music Publications
All Rights Administered by Sony/ATV Music Publishing LLC, 424 Church Street, Suite 1200, Nashville, TN 37219
International Copyright Secured   All Rights Reserved

To Coda ⊕
(End opt. 8va)

D.S. al Coda

CODA

f

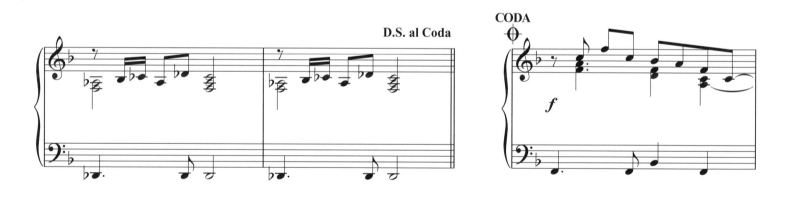

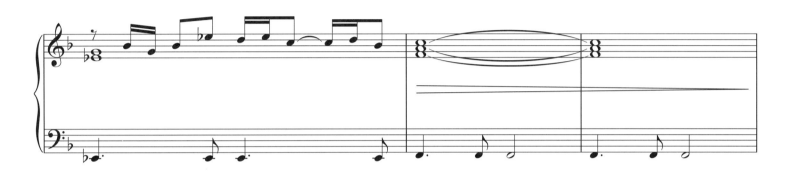

KOKOMO

from the Motion Picture COCKTAIL

Music and Lyrics by JOHN PHILLIPS,
TERRY MELCHER, MIKE LOVE
and SCOTT McKENZIE

Moderately bright

© 1988 Touchstone Pictures Music & Songs, Inc., Spirit Two Music, Inc., Buena Vista Music Company,
Daywin Music, Inc., Clairaudient Music Corporation and Spirit One Music
All Rights Reserved.   Used by Permission.

LEARN TO BE LONELY

from THE PHANTOM OF THE OPERA

Music by ANDREW LLOYD WEBBER
Lyrics by CHARLES HART

© Copyright 2004 Andrew Lloyd Webber licensed to The Really Useful Group Ltd.
International Copyright Secured   All Rights Reserved

LET IT GO
from FROZEN

Music and Lyrics by KRISTEN ANDERSON-LOPEZ
and ROBERT LOPEZ

The snow glows white on the moun-tain to-night; __ not a foot-print __ to be seen. __ A king-dom of i - so-la-

© 2013 Wonderland Music Company, Inc.
All Rights Reserved. Used by Permission.

NOBODY DOES IT BETTER

from THE SPY WHO LOVED ME

Music by MARVIN HAMLISCH
Lyrics by CAROLE BAYER SAGER

© 1977 (Renewed) DANJAQ S.A.
All Rights Administered by EMI U CATALOG INC./EMI UNART CATALOG INC. (Publishing) and ALFRED MUSIC (Print)
All Rights Reserved   Used by Permission

LET THE RIVER RUN

Theme from the Motion Picture WORKING GIRL

Words and Music by
CARLY SIMON

We're com-ing to the edge, run - ning on the wa - ter,

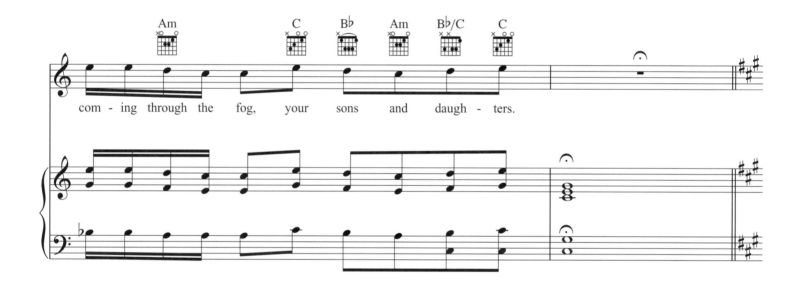

com - ing through the fog, your sons and daugh - ters.

Let the riv - er run, let all the dream - ers wake the

Copyright © 1989 C'est Music and T C F Music Publishing, Inc.
All Rights for C'est Music Administered by BMG Rights Management (US) LLC
All Rights Reserved   Used by Permission

A MAN AND A WOMAN

(Un homme et une femme)

from A MAN AND A WOMAN

Original Words by PIERRE BAROUH
English Words by JERRY KELLER
Music by FRANCIS LAI

When hearts are pass-ing in the night, in the lone-ly night, _____ then they must
si- lence of the mist, of the morn-ing mist, _____ when lips are

hold each oth - er tight, oh, so ver - y tight _____ and take a chance that in the light, in to-
wait-ing to be kissed, long- ing to be kissed, _____ where is the rea - son to re - sist and de-

mor - row's light _____ they'll stay to - geth - er, _____ so much in
ny a kiss _____ that holds a prom - ise _____ of hap - pi-

Copyright © 1966 EDITIONS SARAVAH, Paris, France
Copyright Renewed
All Rights in the U.S. and Canada Controlled and Administered by UNIVERSAL MUSIC CORP.
All Rights Reserved   Used by Permission

MORE
(Ti guarderò nel cuore)
from the film MONDO CANE

Music by NINO OLIVIERO and RIZ ORTOLANI
Italian Lyrics by MARCELLO CIORCIOLINI
English Lyrics by NORMAN NEWELL

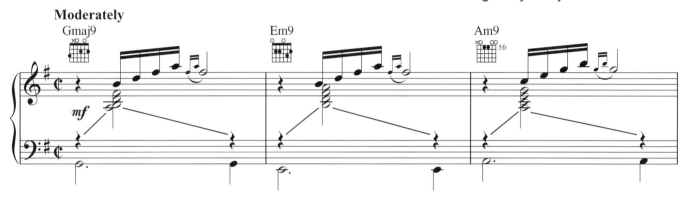

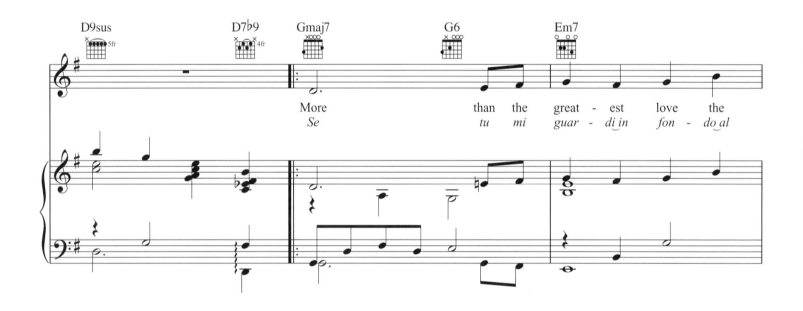

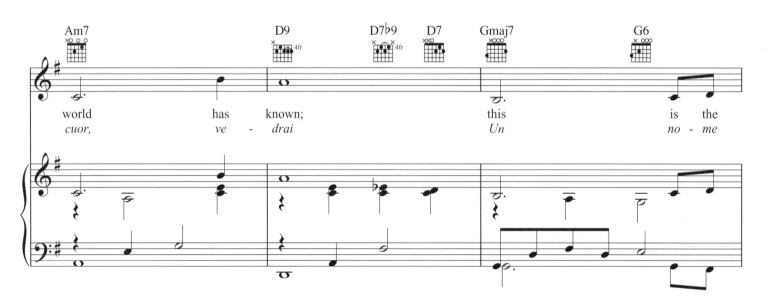

Copyright © 1962 Creazioni Artistiche Musicali C.A.M. S.r.l. and CTC Creative Team Company
Copyright Renewed
International Copyright Secured   All Rights Reserved

THE MUSIC OF GOODBYE

from OUT OF AFRICA

Words and Music by JOHN BARRY,
ALAN BERGMAN and MARILYN BERGMAN

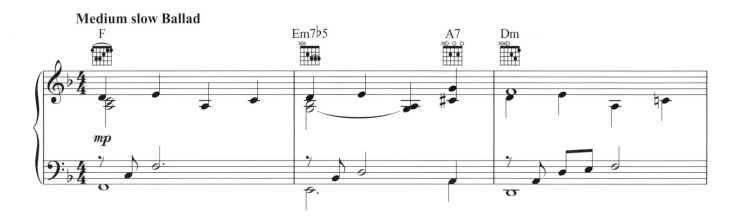

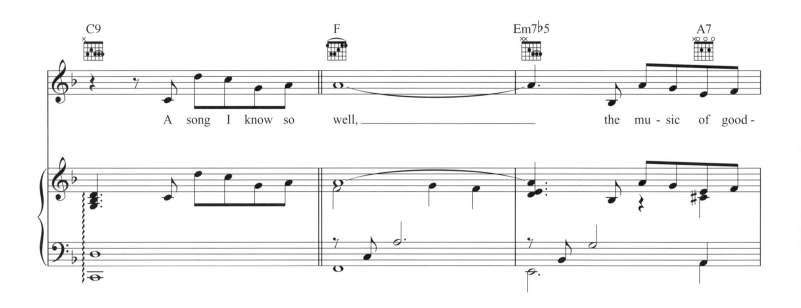

A song I know so well, _____ the mu-sic of good-

bye a-gain. _____ It's there each time we say "Hel-lo." _____

Copyright © 1986 USI B MUSIC PUBLISHING and USI A MUSIC PUBLISHING
All Rights for USI B MUSIC PUBLISHING Administered by SONGS OF UNIVERSAL, INC.
All Rights for USI A MUSIC PUBLISHING Administered by UNIVERSAL MUSIC CORP.
All Rights Reserved   Used by Permission

MY HEART WILL GO ON

(Love Theme from 'Titanic')

from the Paramount and Twentieth Century Fox Motion Picture TITANIC

Music by JAMES HORNER
Lyric by WILL JENNINGS

Copyright © 1997 Sony/ATV Harmony, Sony/ATV Melody, T C F Music Publishing, Inc., Fox Film Music Corporation and Blue Sky Rider Songs
All Rights on behalf of Sony/ATV Harmony and Sony/ATV Melody Administered by Sony/ATV Music Publishing LLC, 424 Church Street, Suite 1200, Nashville, TN 37219
All Rights on behalf of Blue Sky Rider Songs Administered by Irving Music, Inc.
International Copyright Secured   All Rights Reserved

NEVER ON SUNDAY

from Jules Dassin's Motion Picture NEVER ON SUNDAY

Words by BILLY TOWNE
Music by MANOS HADJIDAKIS

Moderately

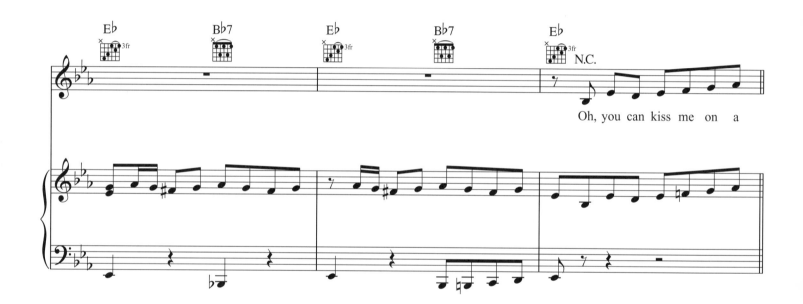

Oh, you can kiss me on a

Mon - day, a Mon - day, a Mon - day is ver - y, ver - y good.
cool day, a hot day, a wet day, which - ev - er one you choose.

© 1960 (Renewed) LLEE CORP. and EMI UNART CATALOG INC.
All Rights for EMI UNART CATALOG INC. Administered by EMI UNART CATALOG INC. (Publishing) and ALFRED MUSIC (Print)
All Rights Reserved

ON GOLDEN POND
Main Theme from ON GOLDEN POND

Music by DAVE GRUSIN

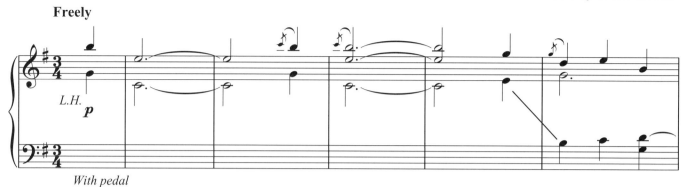

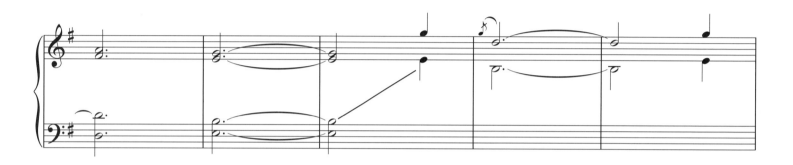

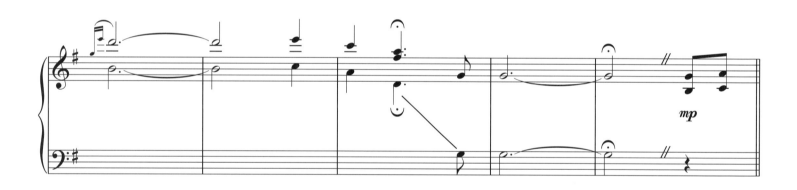

Copyright © 1981 Sony/ATV Music Publishing LLC
All Rights Administered by Sony/ATV Music Publishing LLC, 424 Church Street, Suite 1200, Nashville, TN 37219
International Copyright Secured   All Rights Reserved

OVER THE RAINBOW

from THE WIZARD OF OZ

Music by HAROLD ARLEN
Lyric by E.Y. "YIP" HARBURG

© 1938 (Renewed) METRO-GOLDWYN-MAYER INC.
© 1939 (Renewed) EMI FEIST CATALOG INC.
All Rights Administered by EMI FEIST CATALOG INC. (Publishing) and ALFRED MUSIC (Print)
All Rights Reserved   Used by Permission

fly.   Birds fly   o - ver the rain - bow,   why then, oh why can't

I?   I?

If

hap - py lit - tle blue-birds fly be - yond the rain-bow, why oh why can't   I? _____

QUE SERA, SERA
(Whatever Will Be, Will Be)
from THE MAN WHO KNEW TOO MUCH

Words and Music by JAY LIVINGSTON
and RAYMOND B. EVANS

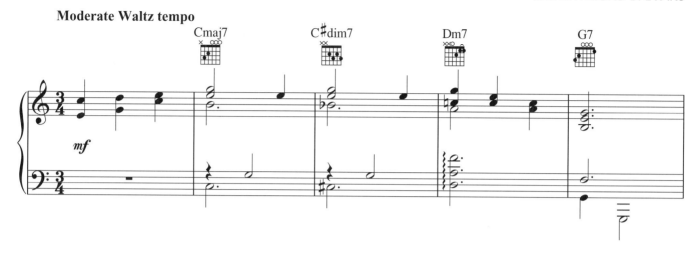

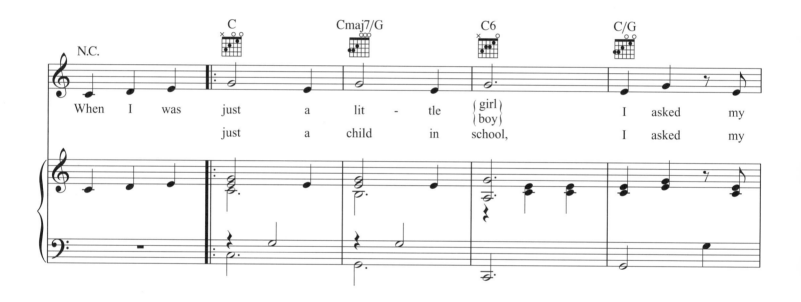

Copyright © 1955 by JAY LIVINGSTON MUSIC and ST. ANGELO MUSIC
Copyright Renewed
All Rights Reserved   Used by Permission

THE RAINBOW CONNECTION
from THE MUPPET MOVIE

Words and Music by PAUL WILLIAMS
and KENNETH L. ASCHER

Moderately, with a lilt

Why are there so man-y songs a-bout rain-bows, and
Who said that ev-'ry wish would be heard and an-swered when

what's on the oth - er side? _____
wished on the morn - ing star? _____

Rain-bows are vi-sions, _ but on-ly il-lu-sions, and
Some-bod - y thought of that, and some-one be-lieved it;

© 1979 Fuzzy Muppet Songs
All Rights Reserved. Used by Permission.

THE ROSE

from the Twentieth Century-Fox Motion Picture Release THE ROSE

Words and Music by
AMANDA McBROOM

© 1977 (Renewed) WARNER-TAMERLANE PUBLISHING CORP. and THIRD STORY MUSIC INC.
All Rights Administered by WARNER-TAMERLANE PUBLISHING CORP.
All Rights Reserved   Used by Permission

SECRET LOVE

from CALAMITY JANE

Words by PAUL FRANCIS WEBSTER
Music by SAMMY FAIN

© 1953 (Renewed) WB MUSIC CORP.
All Rights Reserved   Used by Permission

SEPARATE LIVES
Love Theme from WHITE NIGHTS

Words and Music by
STEPHEN BISHOP

Slowly, freely

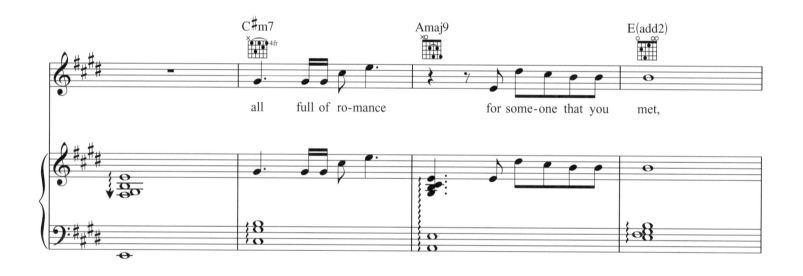

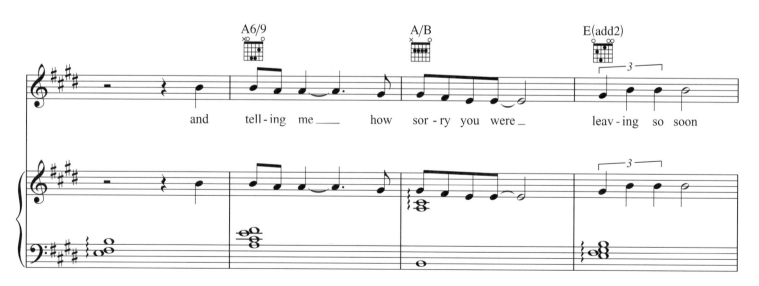

Copyright © 1985 STEPHEN BISHOP MUSIC PUBLISHING, HIT & RUN MUSIC (PUBLISHING) LTD. and EMI GOLD HORIZON MUSIC CORP.
All Rights for STEPHEN BISHOP MUSIC PUBLISHING Administered by UNIVERSAL MUSIC CORP.
All Rights for HIT & RUN MUSIC (PUBLISHING) LTD. Administered by SONY/ATV MUSIC PUBLISHING LLC, 424 Church Street, Suite 1200, Nashville, TN 37219
All Rights Reserved   Used by Permission

SINGIN' IN THE RAIN

from SINGIN' IN THE RAIN

Lyric by ARTHUR FREED
Music by NACIO HERB BROWN

I'm sing - in' in the rain, just sing - in' in the rain. What a

© 1929 (Renewed) METRO-GOLDWYN-MAYER INC.
All Rights Controlled and Administered by EMI ROBBINS CATALOG INC. (Publishing) and ALFRED MUSIC (Print)
All Rights Reserved   Used by Permission

SKYFALL
from the Motion Picture SKYFALL

Words and Music by ADELE ADKINS
and PAUL EPWORTH

Copyright © 2012 MELTED STONE PUBLISHING LTD. and EMI MUSIC PUBLISHING LTD.
All Rights for MELTED STONE PUBLISHING LTD. in the U.S. and Canada Controlled and Administered by UNIVERSAL - SONGS OF POLYGRAM INTERNATIONAL, INC.
All Rights for EMI MUSIC PUBLISHING LTD. Administered by SONY/ATV MUSIC PUBLISHING LLC, 424 Church Street, Suite 1200, Nashville, TN 37219
All Rights Reserved   Used by Permission

SOMEDAY
from THE HUNCHBACK OF NOTRE DAME

Music by ALAN MENKEN
Lyrics by STEPHEN SCHWARTZ

© 1996 Wonderland Music Company, Inc. and Walt Disney Music Company
All Rights Reserved. Used by Permission.

SOMEWHERE IN MY MEMORY
from the Twentieth Century Fox Motion Picture HOME ALONE

Words by LESLIE BRICUSSE
Music by JOHN WILLIAMS

Copyright © 1990 Fox Film Music Corporation and John Hughes Songs
All Rights for John Hughes Songs Administered by Warner-Tamerlane Publishing Corp.
All Rights Reserved   Used by Permission

all of the mu - sic, all of the mag - ic, all of the fam - 'ly

home here with me.

SOMEWHERE OUT THERE

from AN AMERICAN TAIL

Music by BARRY MANN and JAMES HORNER
Lyric by CYNTHIA WEIL

Copyright © 1986 USI A MUSIC PUBLISHING and USI B MUSIC PUBLISHING
All Rights Controlled and Administered by UNIVERSAL MUSIC CORP. and SONGS OF UNIVERSAL, INC.
All Rights Reserved   Used by Permission

through, then we'll be to-geth - er some-where out there, out

where dreams come true.

SOMEWHERE IN TIME

from SOMEWHERE IN TIME

By JOHN BARRY

Moderately slow

Copyright © 1980 USI B GLOBAL MUSIC PUBLISHING
All Rights Controlled and Administered by SONGS OF UNIVERSAL, INC.
All Rights Reserved   Used by Permission

SOONER OR LATER
(I Always Get My Man)
from the Film DICK TRACY

Words and Music by
STEPHEN SONDHEIM

Slow Swing, with a steady beat

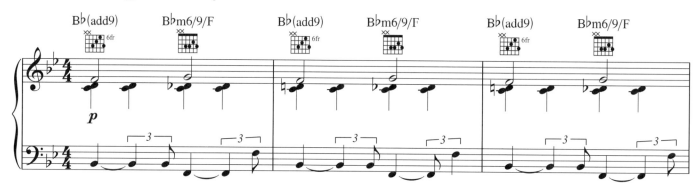

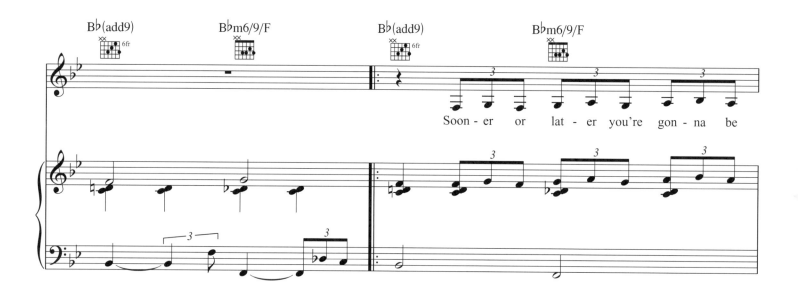

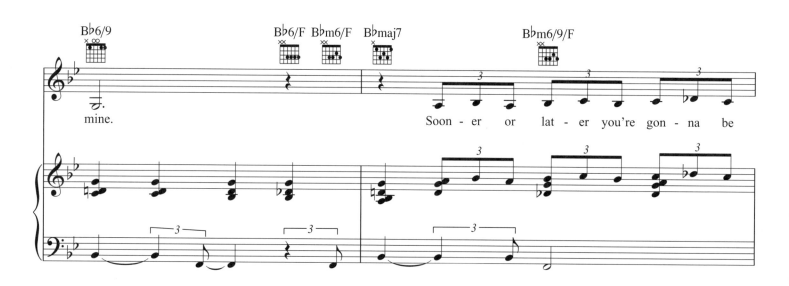

© 1990 RILTING MUSIC, INC. and TOUCHSTONE PICTURES MUSIC AND SONGS, INC.
All Rights for RILTING MUSIC, INC. Administered by WB MUSIC CORP.
All Rights Reserved   Used by Permission

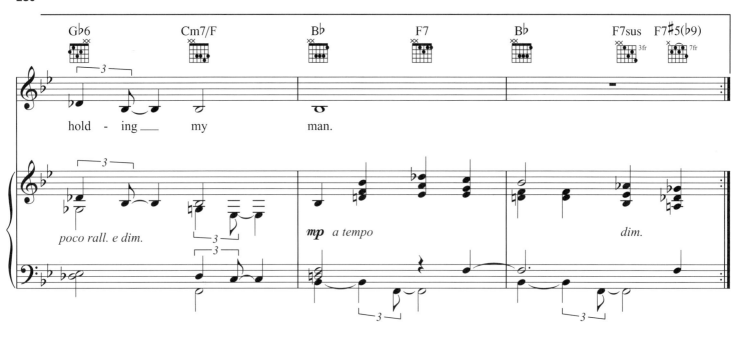

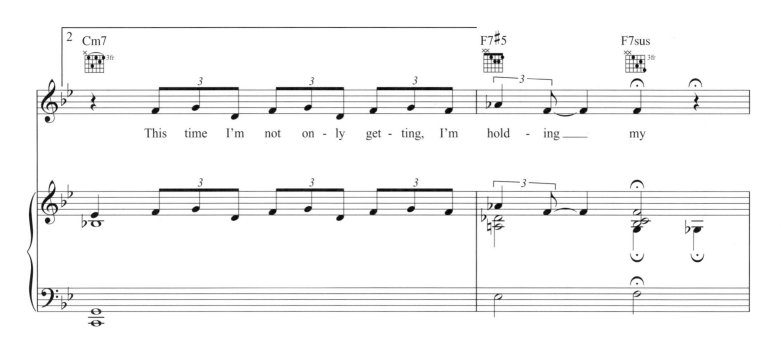

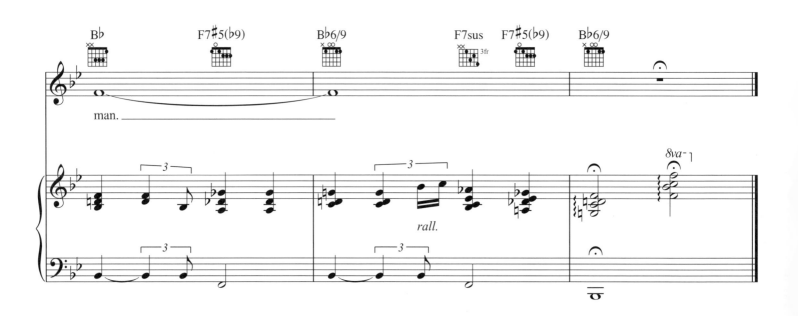

THE SOUND OF MUSIC
from THE SOUND OF MUSIC

Lyrics by OSCAR HAMMERSTEIN II
Music by RICHARD RODGERS

Molto moderato *(tenderly)*

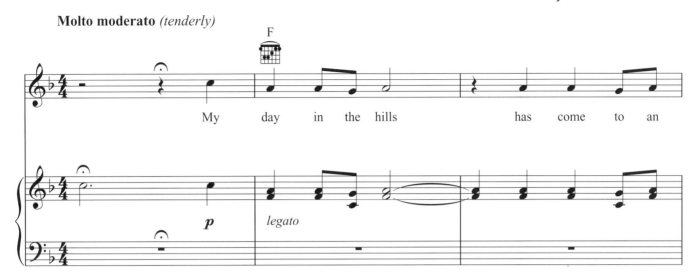

My day in the hills has come to an

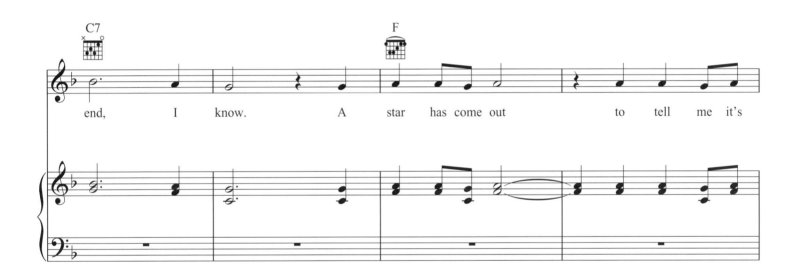

end, I know. A star has come out to tell me it's

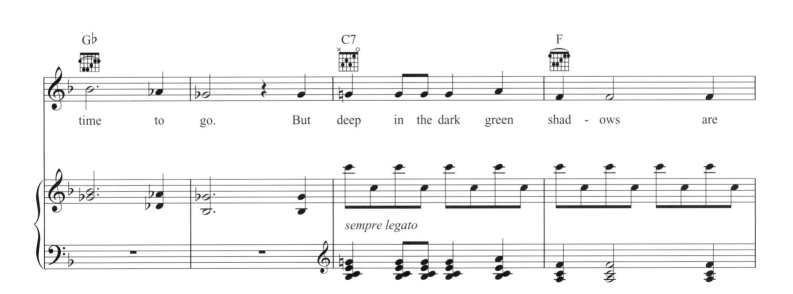

time to go. But deep in the dark green shad-ows are

Copyright © 1959 by Richard Rodgers and Oscar Hammerstein II
Copyright Renewed
Williamson Music, a Division of Rodgers & Hammerstein: an Imagem Company, owner of publication and allied rights throughout the world
International Copyright Secured   All Rights Reserved

284

STAR TREK® THE MOTION PICTURE
Theme from the Paramount Picture STAR TREK: THE MOTION PICTURE

Music by JERRY GOLDSMITH

Moderately fast March tempo

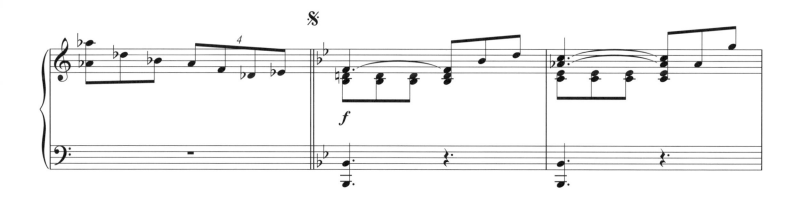

Copyright © 1979 Sony/ATV Music Publishing LLC
All Rights Administered by Sony/ATV Music Publishing LLC, 424 Church Street, Suite 1200, Nashville, TN 37219
International Copyright Secured   All Rights Reserved

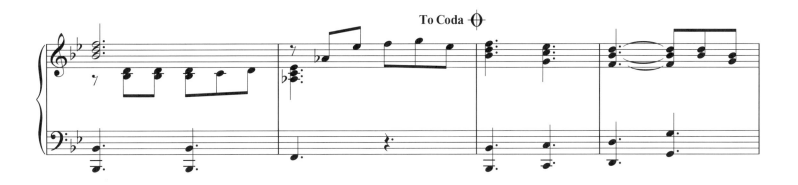

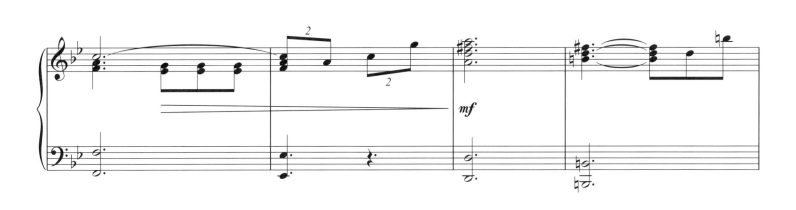

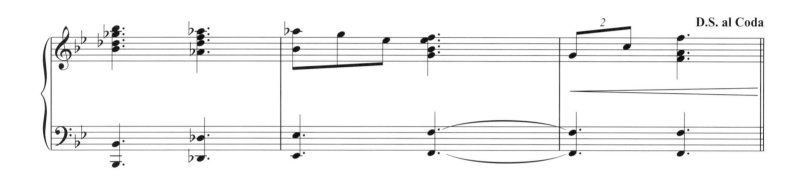

D.S. al Coda

CODA

Slowly, expansively

With pedal

Tempo I

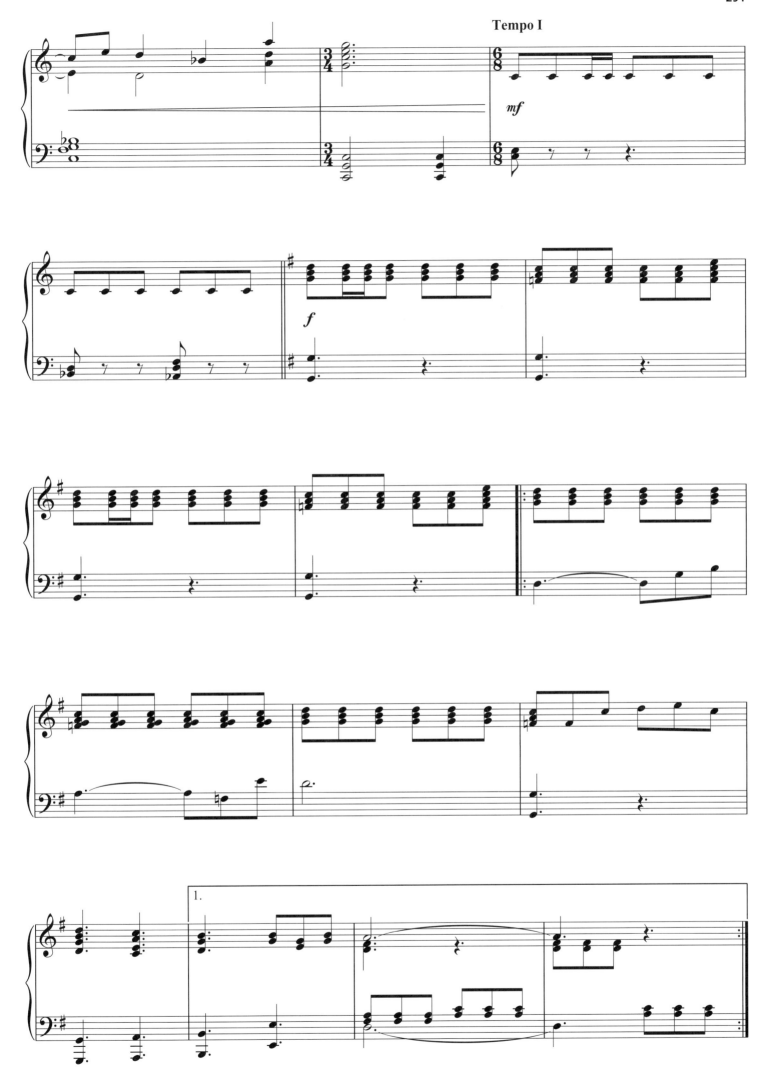

STAYIN' ALIVE
from the Motion Picture SATURDAY NIGHT FEVER

Words and Music by BARRY GIBB,
ROBIN GIBB and MAURICE GIBB

Well, you can tell

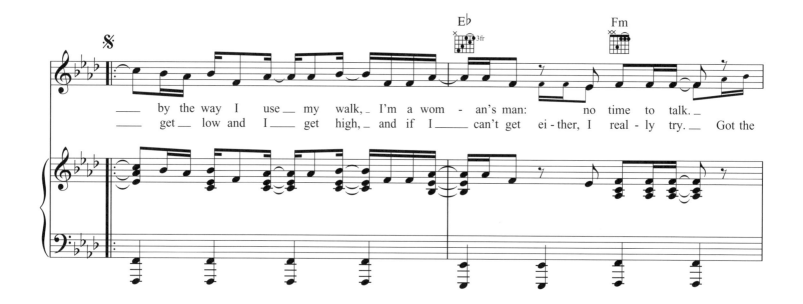

___ by the way I use ___ my walk, ___ I'm a wom - an's man: ___ no time to talk. ___
___ get ___ low and I ___ get high, ___ and if I ___ can't get ei - ther, I ___ real - ly try. ___ Got the

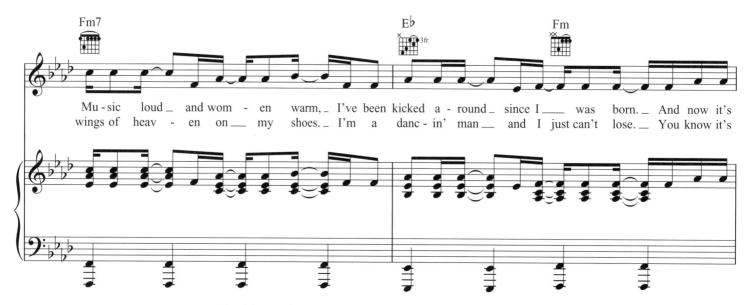

Mu - sic loud ___ and wom - en warm, ___ I've been kicked a - round ___ since I ___ was born. ___ And now it's
wings of heav - en on ___ my shoes. ___ I'm a danc - in' man ___ and I just can't lose. ___ You know it's

Copyright © 1977 by Yvonne Gibb, The Estate Of Robin Gibb and Crompton Songs LLC
Copyright Renewed
All Rights for Yvonne Gibb and The Estate Of Robin Gibb Administered in the U.S. and Canada by Universal Music - Careers
International Copyright Secured   All Rights Reserved

296

TAKE MY BREATH AWAY
(Love Theme)
from the Paramount Picture TOP GUN

Words and Music by GIORGIO MORODER
and TOM WHITLOCK

Moderately slow

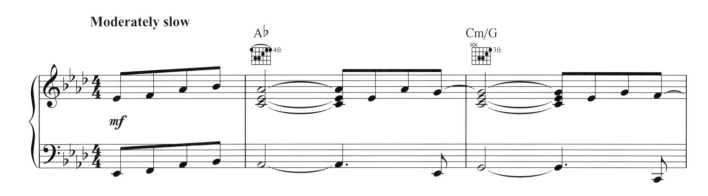

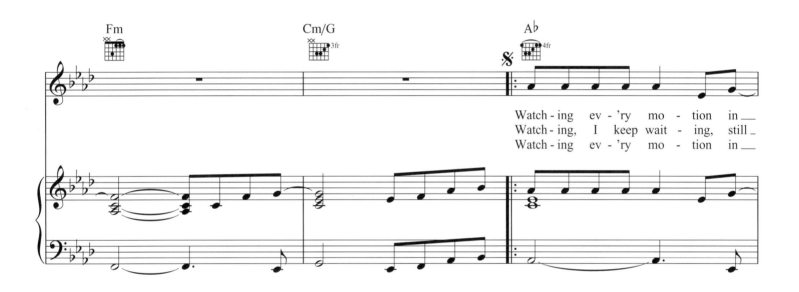

Watch- ing ev - 'ry mo - tion in ___
Watch- ing, I keep wait - ing, still ___
Watch- ing ev - 'ry mo - tion in ___

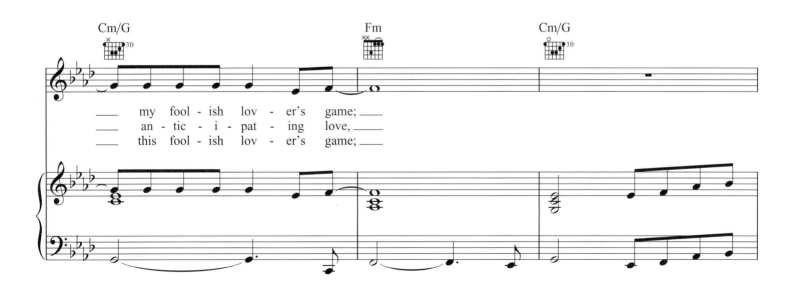

___ my fool - ish lov - er's game; ___
___ an - tic - i - pat - ing love, ___
___ this fool - ish lov - er's game; ___

Copyright © 1986 Sony/ATV Music Publishing LLC and Budde Music, Inc.
All Rights on behalf of Sony/ATV Music Publishing LLC Administered by Sony/ATV Music Publishing LLC, 424 Church Street, Suite 1200, Nashville, TN 37219
All Rights on behalf of Budde Music, Inc. Administered by WB Music Corp.
International Copyright Secured   All Rights Reserved

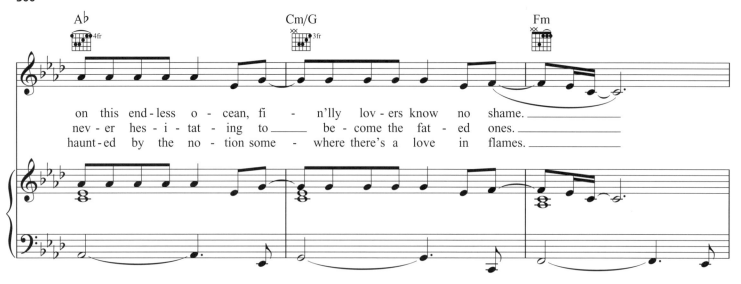

on this end - less o - cean, fi - n'lly lov - ers know no shame. _____
nev - er hes - i - tat - ing to ___ be - come the fat - ed ones. _____
haunt - ed by the no - tion some - where there's a love in flames. _____

Turn - ing and re - turn - ing to _____ some se - cret place in - side; _
Turn - ing and re - turn - ing to _____ some se - cret place to hide; _
Turn - ing and re - turn - ing to _____ some se - cret place in - side; _

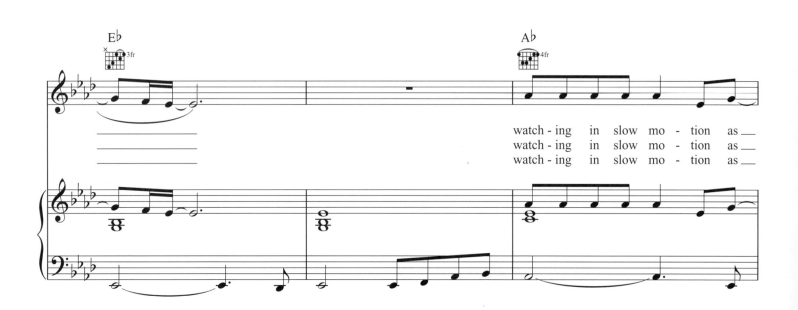

_____ watch - ing in slow mo - tion as __
_____ watch - ing in slow mo - tion as __
_____ watch - ing in slow mo - tion as __

SONG FROM M*A*S*H
(Suicide is Painless)
from M*A*S*H

Words and Music by MIKE ALTMAN
and JOHNNY MANDEL

© 1970 (Renewed) WB MUSIC CORP.
All Rights Reserved   Used by Permission

Additional Lyrics

2. The game of life is hard to play,
I'm going to lose it anyway,
The losing card I'll someday lay,
So this is all I have to say,
(Chorus)

3. The sword of time will pierce our skins,
It doesn't hurt when it begins
But as it works its way on in,
The pain grows stronger, watch it grin
(Chorus)

4. A brave man once requested me
To answer questions that are key,
Is it to be or not to be
And I replied; "Oh, why ask me,"
(Chorus)

THEME FROM SUMMER OF '42
(The Summer Knows)
Theme from SUMMER OF '42

Music by MICHEL LEGRAND

Slowly

© 1971 (Renewed) WARNER-OLIVE MUSIC LLC
All Rights Administered by UNIVERSAL MUSIC GROUP
Exclusive Worldwide Print Rights Administered by ALFRED MUSIC
All Rights Reserved   Used by Permission

THREE COINS IN THE FOUNTAIN

from THREE COINS IN THE FOUNTAIN

Words by SAMMY CAHN
Music by JULE STYNE

© 1954 (Renewed) PRODUCERS MUSIC PUBLISHING CO., INC. and CAHN MUSIC COMPANY
All Rights for PRODUCERS MUSIC PUBLISHING CO., INC. in the U.S. and Canada Administered by CHAPPELL & CO., INC.
Worldwide Rights for CAHN MUSIC COMPANY in the U.S. and Canada Administered by IMAGEM SOUNDS
All Rights Reserved   Used by Permission

309

THE TROLLEY SONG
from MEET ME IN ST. LOUIS

Words and Music by HUGH MARTIN
and RALPH BLANE

© 1943 (Renewed) METRO-GOLDWYN-MAYER INC.
© 1944 (Renewed) EMI FEIST CATALOG INC.
All Rights Controlled by EMI FEIST CATALOG INC. (Publishing) and ALFRED MUSIC (Print)
All Rights Reserved   Used by Permission

TOMORROW
from the Musical Production ANNIE

Lyric by MARTIN CHARNIN
Music by CHARLES STROUSE

Moderately slow

© 1977 (Renewed) EDWIN H. MORRIS & COMPANY, A Division of MPL Music Publishing, Inc. and CHARLES STROUSE PUBLISHING
All Rights for CHARLES STROUSE PUBLISHING Administered by WB MUSIC CORP.
All Rights Reserved   Used by Permission

UNCHAINED MELODY

from the Motion Picture UNCHAINED
featured in the Motion Picture GHOST

Lyric by HY ZARET
Music by ALEX NORTH

© 1955 (Renewed) North Melody Publishing (SESAC) and HZUM Publishing (SESAC) c/o Unchained Melody Publishing, LLC
All Rights Reserved   Used by Permission

THE WAY YOU LOOK TONIGHT

from SWING TIME

featured in the TriStar Motion Picture MY BEST FRIEND'S WEDDING

Words by DOROTHY FIELDS
Music by JEROME KERN

Copyright © 1936 UNIVERSAL - POLYGRAM INTERNATIONAL PUBLISHING, INC. and ALDI MUSIC
Copyright Renewed
Print Rights for ALDI MUSIC in the U.S. Controlled and Administered by HAPPY ASPEN MUSIC LLC c/o SHAPIRO, BERNSTEIN & CO., INC.
All Rights Reserved   Used by Permission

UNDER THE SEA
from THE LITTLE MERMAID

Music by ALAN MENKEN
Lyrics by HOWARD ASHMAN

The sea-weed is al-ways green-er
Down here __ all the fish is hap-py

in some-bod-y else-'s lake.
as off __ through the waves dey roll.

You dream __ a-bout
The fish __ on the

© 1988 Wonderland Music Company, Inc. and Walt Disney Music Company
All Rights Reserved. Used by Permission.

oh, that blow - fish blow.

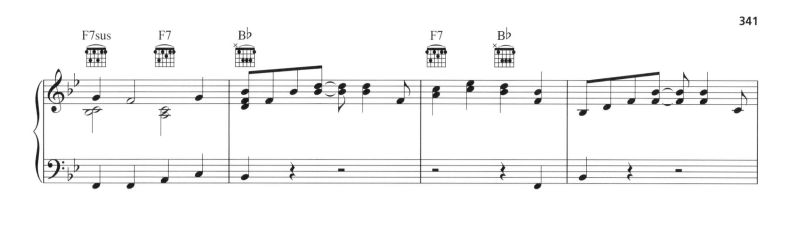

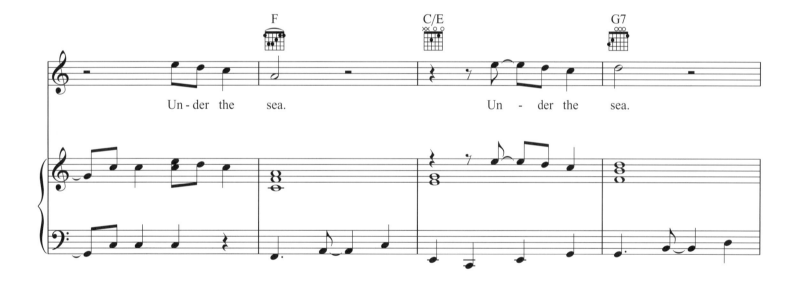

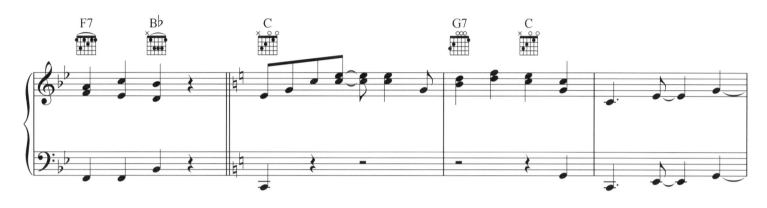

Un-der the   sea.   Un - der the   sea.

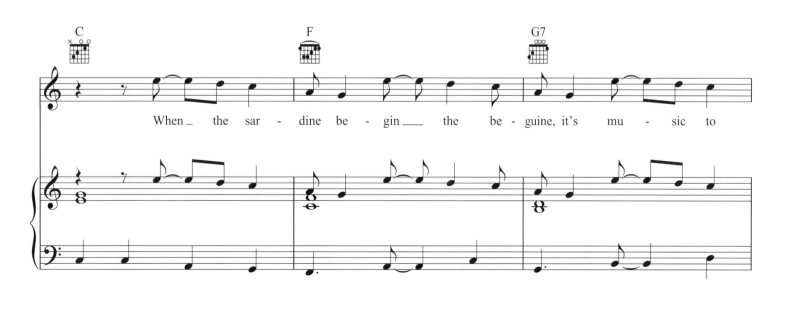

When _ the sar - dine be - gin _ the   be - guine, it's mu - sic to

WHAT A WONDERFUL WORLD

featured in the Motion Picture GOOD MORNING VIETNAM

Words and Music by GEORGE DAVID WEISS
and BOB THIELE

Copyright © 1967 by Range Road Music Inc., Quartet Music and Abilene Music, Inc.
Copyright Renewed
All Rights for Quartet Music Administered by BMG Rights Management (US) LLC
All Rights for Abilene Music, Inc. Administered Worldwide by Imagem Music LLC
International Copyright Secured   All Rights Reserved
Used by Permission

YELLOW SUBMARINE

from YELLOW SUBMARINE

Words and Music by JOHN LENNON
and PAUL McCARTNEY

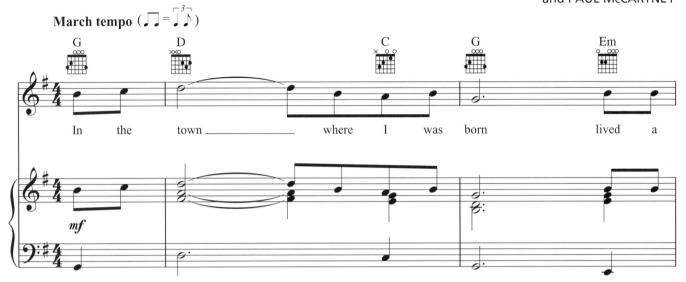

In the town where I was born lived a

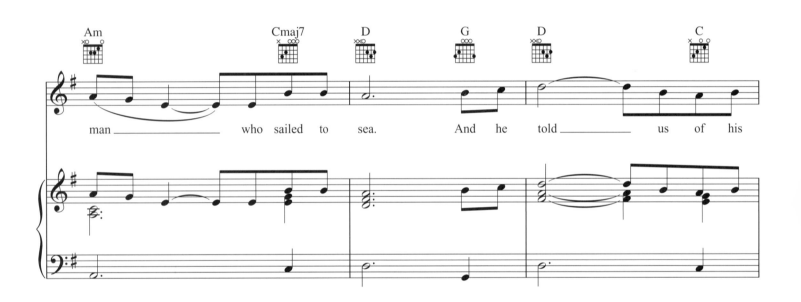

man who sailed to sea. And he told us of his

life in the land of sub - ma - rines. So we

Copyright © 1966 Sony/ATV Music Publishing LLC
Copyright Renewed
All Rights Administered by Sony/ATV Music Publishing LLC, 424 Church Street, Suite 1200, Nashville, TN 37219
International Copyright Secured   All Rights Reserved

YOU'VE GOT A FRIEND IN ME

from TOY STORY

Music and Lyrics by
RANDY NEWMAN

You've got a friend in me.
You've got a friend in me.

You've got a friend in me.
You've got a friend in me.

When the road looks rough a-head and you're miles
You got trou-bles, then I got 'em, too.

© 1995 Walt Disney Music Company
All Rights Reserved. Used by Permission.

ZIP-A-DEE-DOO-DAH
from SONG OF THE SOUTH

Words by RAY GILBERT
Music by ALLIE WRUBEL

Moderately fast

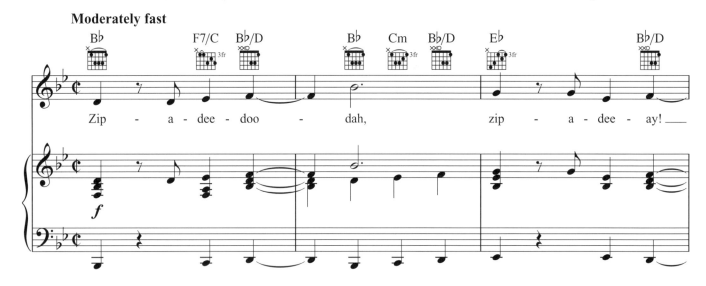

Zip - a - dee - doo - dah, zip - a - dee - ay! ___

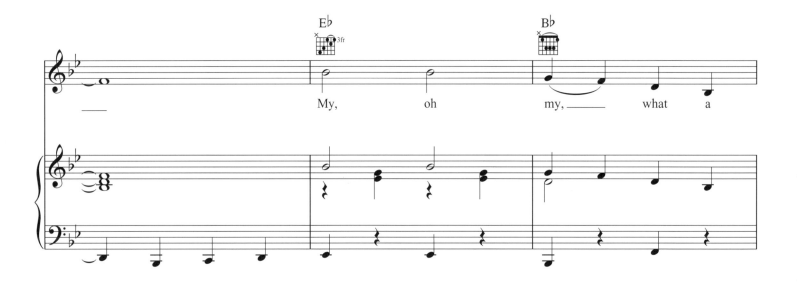

___ My, oh my, ___ what a

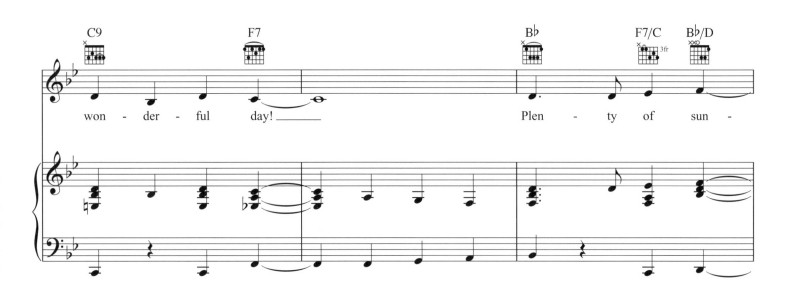

won - der - ful day! ___ Plen - ty of sun -

© 1945 Walt Disney Music Company
Copyright Renewed.
All Rights Reserved. Used by Permission.

BIG BOOKS of Music

Our "Big Books" feature big selections of popular titles under one cover, perfect for performing musicians, music aficionados or the serious hobbyist. All books are arranged for piano, voice, and guitar, and feature stay-open binding, so the books lie flat without breaking the spine.

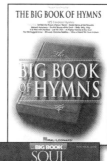

BIG BOOK OF BALLADS – 2ND ED.
62 songs.
00310485 .... $19.95

BIG BOOK OF BIG BAND HITS
84 songs.
00310701 .... $22.99

BIG BOOK OF BLUEGRASS SONGS
70 songs.
00311484 .... $19.95

BIG BOOK OF BLUES
80 songs.
00311843 .... $19.99

BIG BOOK OF BROADWAY
70 songs.
00311658 .... $22.99

BIG BOOK OF CHILDREN'S SONGS
55 songs.
00359261 .... $16.99

GREAT BIG BOOK OF CHILDREN'S SONGS
76 songs.
00310002 .... $15.99

BIG BOOK OF CHRISTMAS SONGS – 2ND ED.
126 songs.
00311520 .... $19.95

BIG BOOK OF CLASSICAL MUSIC
100 songs.
00310508 .... $19.99

BIG BOOK OF CONTEMPORARY CHRISTIAN FAVORITES – 3RD ED.
50 songs.
00312067 .... $21.99

BIG BOOK OF '50s & '60s SWINGING SONGS
67 songs.
00310982 .... $19.95

BIG BOOK OF FOLKSONGS
125 songs.
00312549 .... $19.99

BIG BOOK OF FRENCH SONGS
70 songs.
00311154 .... $19.95

BIG BOOK OF GERMAN SONGS
78 songs.
00311816 .... $19.99

BIG BOOK OF GOSPEL SONGS
100 songs.
00310604 .... $19.95

BIG BOOK OF HYMNS
125 hymns.
00310510 .... $19.99

BIG BOOK OF IRISH SONGS
76 songs.
00310981 .... $19.99

BIG BOOK OF ITALIAN FAVORITES
80 songs.
00311185 .... $19.99

BIG BOOK OF JAZZ – 2ND ED.
75 songs.
00311557 .... $22.99

BIG BOOK OF LATIN AMERICAN SONGS
89 songs.
00311562 .... $19.95

BIG BOOK OF MOTOWN
84 songs.
00311061 .... $19.95

BIG BOOK OF NOSTALGIA
158 songs.
00310004 .... $24.99

BIG BOOK OF OLDIES
73 songs.
00310756 .... $19.95

THE BIG BOOK OF PRAISE & WORSHIP
52 songs.
00140795 .... $22.99

BIG BOOK OF RAGTIME PIANO
63 songs.
00311749 .... $19.95

BIG BOOK OF SOUL
71 songs.
00310771 .... $19.95

BIG BOOK OF STANDARDS
86 songs.
00311667 .... $19.95

BIG BOOK OF SWING
84 songs.
00310359 .... $19.95

BIG BOOK OF TORCH SONGS – 2ND ED.
75 songs.
00310561 .... $19.99

BIG BOOK OF TV THEME SONGS
78 songs.
00310504 .... $19.95

BIG BOOK OF WEDDING MUSIC
77 songs.
00311567 .... $22.99

Prices, contents, and availability subject to change without notice.

Visit **www.halleonard.com**
for our entire catalog and to view our complete songlists.

0218

THE NEW DECADE SERIES

 Books with Online Audio • Arranged for Piano, Voice, and Guitar

The New Decade Series features collections of iconic songs from each decade with great backing tracks so you can play them and sound like a pro. You access the tracks online for streaming or download. **See complete song listings online at www.halleonard.com**

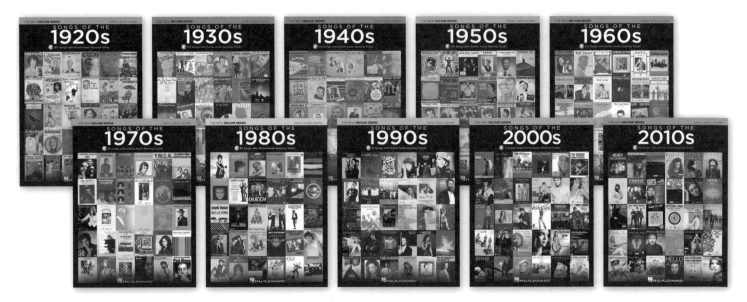

SONGS OF THE 1920s
Ain't Misbehavin' • Baby Face • California, Here I Come • Fascinating Rhythm • I Wanna Be Loved by You • It Had to Be You • Mack the Knife • Ol' Man River • Puttin' on the Ritz • Rhapsody in Blue • Someone to Watch over Me • Tea for Two • Who's Sorry Now • and more.
00137576 P/V/G...................................$24.99

SONGS OF THE 1930s
As Time Goes By • Blue Moon • Cheek to Cheek • Embraceable You • A Fine Romance • Georgia on My Mind • I Only Have Eyes for You • The Lady Is a Tramp • On the Sunny Side of the Street • Over the Rainbow • Pennies from Heaven • Stormy Weather (Keeps Rainin' All the Time) • The Way You Look Tonight • and more.
00137579 P/V/G...................................$24.99

SONGS OF THE 1940s
At Last • Boogie Woogie Bugle Boy • Don't Get Around Much Anymore • God Bless' the Child • How High the Moon • It Could Happen to You • La Vie En Rose (Take Me to Your Heart Again) • Route 66 • Sentimental Journey • The Trolley Song • You'd Be So Nice to Come Home To • Zip-A-Dee-Doo-Dah • and more.
00137582 P/V/G...................................$24.99

SONGS OF THE 1950s
Ain't That a Shame • Be-Bop-A-Lula • Chantilly Lace • Earth Angel • Fever • Great Balls of Fire • Love Me Tender • Mona Lisa • Peggy Sue • Que Sera, Sera (Whatever Will Be, Will Be) • Rock Around the Clock • Sixteen Tons • A Teenager in Love • That'll Be the Day • Unchained Melody • Volare • You Send Me • Your Cheatin' Heart • and more.
00137595 P/V/G...................................$24.99

SONGS OF THE 1960s
All You Need Is Love • Beyond the Sea • Born to Be Wild • California Girls • Dancing in the Street • Happy Together • King of the Road • Leaving on a Jet Plane • Louie, Louie • My Generation • Oh, Pretty Woman • Sunshine of Your Love • Under the Boardwalk • You Really Got Me • and more.
00137596 P/V/G $24.99

SONGS OF THE 1970s
ABC • Bridge over Troubled Water • Cat's in the Cradle • Dancing Queen • Free Bird • Goodbye Yellow Brick Road • Hotel California • I Will Survive • Joy to the World • Killing Me Softly with His Song • Layla • Let It Be • Piano Man • The Rainbow Connection • Stairway to Heaven • The Way We Were • Your Song • and more.
00137599 P/V/G $27.99

SONGS OF THE 1980s
Addicted to Love • Beat It • Careless Whisper • Come on Eileen • Don't Stop Believin' • Every Rose Has Its Thorn • Footloose • I Just Called to Say I Love You • Jessie's Girl • Livin' on a Prayer • Saving All My Love for You • Take on Me • Up Where We Belong • The Wind Beneath My Wings • and more.
00137600 P/V/G $27.99

SONGS OF THE 1990s
Angel • Black Velvet • Can You Feel the Love Tonight • (Everything I Do) I Do It for You • Friends in Low Places • Hero • I Will Always Love You • More Than Words • My Heart Will Go On (Love Theme from 'Titanic') • Smells like Teen Spirit • Under the Bridge • Vision of Love • Wonderwall • and more.
00137601 P/V/G $27.99

SONGS OF THE 2000s
Bad Day • Beautiful • Before He Cheats • Chasing Cars • Chasing Pavements • Drops of Jupiter (Tell Me) • Fireflies • Hey There Delilah • How to Save a Life • I Gotta Feeling • I'm Yours • Just Dance • Love Story • 100 Years • Rehab • Unwritten • You Raise Me Up • and more.
00137608 P/V/G $27.99

SONGS OF THE 2010s
All About That Bass • All of Me • Brave • Empire State of Mind • Get Lucky • Happy • Hey, Soul Sister • I Knew You Were Trouble • Just the Way You Are • Need You Now • Pompeii • Radioactive • Rolling in the Deep • Shake It Off • Shut up and Dance • Stay with Me • Take Me to Church • Thinking Out Loud • Uptown Funk • and many more.
00151836 P/V/G $27.99

 HAL•LEONARD®

halleonard.com
Prices, content, and availability subject to change without notice.

0317